Coping with Emotions and Otters

Coping
with Emotions
and Otters

Dina Del Bucchia

To Shirley,
You're lovely!
Robson Square Forever!
xo

Talonbooks

© 2013 by Dina Del Bucchia

Talonbooks
P.O. Box 2076, Vancouver, British Columbia, Canada V6B 3S3
www.talonbooks.com

Typeset in Adobe Garamond
Printed and bound in Canada on SFI-certified paper
Cover painting: *Otters Holding Hands*, Lesley DeSantis, www.whenguineapigsfly.com
Cover and interior design by Typesmith

First printing: 2013

The publisher gratefully acknowledges the financial support of the Canada Council
for the Arts, the Government of Canada through the Canada Book Fund, and the
Province of British Columbia through the British Columbia Arts Council and the
Book Publishing Tax Credit for our publishing activities.

LIBRARY AND ARCHIVES CANADA CATALOGUING IN PUBLICATION

Del Bucchia, Dina, 1979–
    Coping with emotions and otters / Dina Del Bucchia.

Poems.

Also issued in electronic format.

ISBN 978-0-88922-764-4

    I. Title.

PS8607.E482538C66 2013   C811'.6   C2013-900194-8

For my parents

Emotional
OUTLETS

I bought this book. I read it. But still, no one listens to me. I just sit there. I tried doing what the book said. Smiling. Shouting. Glad-handing. Patting men on the back. But I'm no good at it. This book is premised on the suggestion that it will help you. Well, it sure didn't help me. I am so sad and lonely. The book made me feel even more isolated. Maybe this book will help you, but it didn't help me. Worse than before. Sad. Lost.

– Mathias Arnold III, Chicago, Illinois
  Amazon.ca customer review posted December 7, 2000,
  commenting on *How to Win Friends and Influence People*
  by Dale Carnegie

HOW TO
be Jealous

Jealousy. Seems easy, right? But do you really understand its power and potential? Are you really sure that what you're experiencing is jealousy? Take the quiz below.

1. *Do other people have stuff you want?*

2. *Do you covet in your sleep?*

3. *Do you ever claim not to be jealous?*

If you answered "yes" or said "maybe" to any of these questions, that's super and confirms that jealousy lives inside you. But how can jealousy enhance your life? With careful administration of the easy-to-follow steps in this guide, you too can become a *Master of Jealousy*.

1.

Take a friend's mother out
to lunch at that place
she always pines for –
rustic bread, sharp dill,
clotted spreads. Talk
about things she loves –
weekends away, popular
news anchors, other people's
problems. Pretend your friend
is the one who forgot to feed the fish,
forgot to vote, forgot
to mail a birthday card
to her own grandmother.
Use your friend's name
only in reference
to recent sex
crimes.

2.

Combine pollen, black
pepper, paint chips, rain.
Create a signature scent,
perfume that strips others
of strong, personal aromas
but makes you irresistible,
impossible for anyone
to resist, to inhale
like spring buds.

3.

Wear your oldest pair
of underwear, saved from high school
in a drawer with braided
jewellery, wallet-sized photos
of you before shit broke
you down, before you
realized these underwear
would help you cling
to a body
you hated.

4.

Tear through town. Root up
roads with bare hands, scatter
concrete. Loiter in crosswalks
until a convertible pulls up.
Bite your cheek,
send a message,
saliva and blood
soak the back seat.

5.

Betray a dolphin.

6.

Redefine jealousy without words.
Draw abstract cartoons
on office walls, sticks for men
who risk nothing, hard circles
for tepid women. Conceal them
with petal-pink stickies.

7.

Be obvious. Stalk bar stools,
succumb to even the weakest
pickups. Collect phone numbers,
encounters, orgasms. Keep a record,
tape it to your front door.

8.

Carve into saplings, snap
pea shoots, shave puppies,
insult fetuses. Damage
and slander anything
younger than you.
Write a treatise
on the false virtue of virility.
Visit elementary schools,
finger paint the hell
out of everything.
Cover your work
with gold stars.

REGISTRY

I scour gift registries for old boyfriends, a name, picture the face of a fiancée, symmetrical, pure skin, doubly-pierced ears. In my head, the woman wears an apron, even though, most likely, she lives in fleece, cooks in jeans and expensive socks, no bra, ponytailed hair, for now, before she has to cut if off, keep it short to become a better wife. I go over the items, deciding if the stainless steel describes the way she makes him feel, makes him push her to call in sick for sex. If she chooses Cuisinart over KitchenAid, she must have rounded nails. If she prefers Jamie Oliver to Gordon Ramsay, there is no way she likes it rough. Already having a whisk means they'll be divorced in less than a year. Sheets for a double bed make them either horny or furious. Patterned china means they're soulmates. A man once surprised me with a giant mug on Valentine's Day, and even though we weren't dating, I took it as a sign that we could be. Something so large and ceramic showed me the container for love could come in any form. We didn't even kiss. I forgot he was dating my cousin. I don't make lists of what I want. I prefer to be taken aback, wowed, shamed. I prefer to be disappointed with what I don't have.

WHEN A *lap* is a CHAIR

A living room becomes the cab of a pickup truck, a tight spot. The space between a man's knees narrows, is interrupted by an ass, sharp as a quarry. She lounges, simpers, giggles, and he tries to keep things balanced. The weight of a girl so slight can devastate a party. She insults the dip, won't take a bite, waits on us to serve her appletinis, takes the conversation, shoos it away. The lap becomes invisible, reappears, a new structure. We see the velour of a second-hand sofa, the cushion of a tweed Hide-A-Bed, Scotchgard. We all want to climb into the back of a real truck and drive away. Instead we pick her up, press her into a ball, roll out creases, round harsh edges. Him, we take apart, from lap to ankle, head to waist. Cushion by cushion, we set the pieces on their sides, fit them together in the most comfortable way, build a fort, climb inside with our ball to play.

Shame *Affirmations*

If you still question your commitment to shame or are unsure if you have enough built up inside you, don't be discouraged. The following suggested shame affirmations should provide even the proudest person with a stockpile of deep humiliation that will last for months, perhaps even years. Repeat these affirmations in the order in which they are listed; then try mixing them up. Eventually, you'll find the right way because one does indeed exist. There is always a wrong way.

①
I will save each grey hair
I shed in the glass box
reserved for love tokens.

②
I will admit I was the one who peed
in the sandbox in grades 2 and 4.

③
I will strive to achieve a better
credit rating and fail.

④
I will eat burnt dinner while
watching the Weather Network.

⑤
I will hold my dreams
close to my heart.

⑥
I will salvage my discards
from the dumpster.

⑦
I will reveal one secret
fantasy per week.

⑧
I will try to impress the smart
woman at the Whole Foods
deli with my knowledge
of fantasy football.

⑨
I will fish for compliments until
a friend excuses herself.

⑩
I will examine my failings,
each weakness documented
in my shame journal.

⑪
I will wonder how I survive.

HOW to
be *Ashamed*

Why are we so afraid of shame? The feeling that heats our chest and cheeks is powerful, and if used at full force has the ability to make us better people. Don't hide from your shame. Don't put it in a drawer with your lost dreams, catalogue clippings, soggy matchbooks, and expired condoms and allow it to turn to clutter. Allow it to blossom. Once you take this emotion seriously, you'll be rewarded with a bouquet of flourishing shame.

1.

Return to your elementary school,
squat on tiny toilets, wash
your hands next to fresh,
sticky six-year-olds. Compare your
withered skin to theirs,
abundant elastin, ignorant.
Look down and see
their hopeful heads
level with your pocket full
of bland business cards
flat to hip, slated to unimpress.
Rectangles of paper
no one asks about
anymore.

2.

Create a crossword
about your life, memories
blissful, all elation, significant
moments that would suit
a personalized greeting card.
Watch your loved ones
struggle to fill numbered blocks –
unsure of specific reasons
you experience joy.

3.

Remain calm.
Shame will most likely
come to you, worm in
on the lips of a friend,
the shade of summer,
repulsion and rejection.
Welcome it.

4.

Use public transportation
to move small items
to a new home. Tote
expired dairy products,
used toothbrushes,
soiled rags, useless
lint roller. Make multiple trips
to expose your meagre life
to as many strangers as possible.

5.

Make copies of your prom photos,
cut them into geometric shapes,
each inscribed with notes, secret
shames. Attach comment cards,
a return address, a sliver of skin.
At lunchtime on a clear day,
climb to the roof of a building
where you were let go
for working too slowly,
scatter your photo-
       graphic
            confetti,
wait.

6.

Talk politics
with your secret crush,
catch the glint of uncertainty
as you mispronounce countries,
movements, quote publications
that don't exist. Listen
to the rebuttal, shake your head,
agree, then make the same mistakes
all over again. Watch
a nervous check of time,
mutter excuses. Fumble
for common ground, connectivity.
It's not that you don't agree,
just that you're so oblivious
you can't even change the subject.

7.

Take Paxil daily
while you stand at the water cooler.
Ease the pill down your throat,
tell everyone, *These pills!*
These horse pills, these horse pills,
these candy-coated chokers.
Wife makes me take 'em
all for her, worried
about my ticker. Heart disease
is relatable, builds bonds.
Though you know
your co-workers
have you figured out,
persist with this lie.

8.

Closely follow
a reality TV competition,
add the number
of your chosen competitor
to your phone's favourites. Ignore
your unpaid bills. Each week
scrutinize the dancers, singers,
chefs, and models.
When your favourite is voted off,
create a Fan Page,
become friends with preteens
who share your interests.
When confronted, pretend
your devotion is a joke.

QUEUED *up*

That man is so fat, says the child, burrows a gummy face into the artful layers of his mother's outfit. She doesn't scold, look as though this little boy, too big to be carried, is wrong. With a delicate hand, she brushes his hair, cradles him, presses love to his forehead. At the front of the line, the man can't hear. He pays, chats up the baristas, leans into the counter, smooths his hands over the roundness of his belly, laughs at a joke no one told, tells the baristas he is very thirsty this morning, for brunettes in aprons. *I want two of the chocolate things,* the child yells, points, busts a fist into his cheek. His mother whispers, his pink ear almost in her mouth, *Do you want to be fat, sweetie?* I wish she was lumpy, stained, would unravel by frayed threads on the plywood-flat ass of her bra-like yoga pants. I wish there was shame. I could open my mouth, tell them this is a civilized place, but I nudge past the fat man and the woman, politely order coffee to go.

Battery TEST

Try to locate a lost toy, the kind that looks stuffed on the outside, rooted hard-plastic innards, the kind that move in stilted gait, horror-movie whirring sounds. Bark, purr, growl, squeak, beep. Like you, a man in an office had ideas about the toy, without knowing how they would play out in a child's bedroom, that an adult would pine to hear sounds he created. Noise for something he didn't know the shape of, a clattering loop. Dress like that man, short-sleeved button-up, too-short tie, flat-brown slacks, with a line of ballpoint blue mid-thigh. The sounds are jumbled in your head. You search for them as you search for the toy. Was it an elephant, a puppy, a bunny? Envision your mouth as a cavern for sound. Practise remembering the sounds, the toy. Make noises that vibrate your teeth, cut down to your navel. Spend weeks testing batteries. Anticipate a reunion.

HOW *to* ^{be}**Angry**

Anger is a very powerful emotion. How can you make it work in your favour? It's easy to throw a plate, smash a beloved tchotchke, or even give the finger. Don't you want to stand out in a crowd? It's your chance. Make your anger your best anger yet. Heck, make it anyone's best anger. Make it the best, most useful, most awesome in the world. In the following handy ten-step guide, you will learn how to explore the further reaches of anger, and how to get in touch with your most inner, most personal, most angry self.

1.

Clear your throat to be heard
above the Food Network reruns.
Julia Child's breasts and apron almost
touching, her voice, reverberating from
beyond the grave, reaches its highest
octave of instruction, *Marinate the quail!*

Forget about hot dogs, pop, and chips. Forget.
That time is over. Listen to this giant
woman, quiver in her voice, control in her filet.
Chopping blocks can be perfectly messy, things
can be difficult. Forget the yellow puffs
that spring into chickens.

Terror comes from the blade of a knife through
a convex screen – and that apron
could strap you in, bind you. Put down
your empty bowl, clean spoon, acknowledge
that you haven't cooked a thing. Change
the channel seven clicks on the remote
control.

2.

Always keep your empty
to-go cups in cup holders,
then claim they're full
when someone asks
to throw them out,
to put their own
scalding wake-up call
in a secure spot. Weave in
and out of the car-pool lane,
cut off buses. Think
about the verb "jostle."
Memorize cross-
word clues to mutter
while circling the barricaded city blocks
until construction ceases. Your regular spot
is available, but a squirrel
died there.
Back in quickly.

3.

Before bed, make quick, jarring motions
as you jump off the couch. Brush your top teeth only,
then burrow under the covers. Roll in them
until all you've left is a bare flat sheet
for someone else to freeze on.

4.

Refuse to work through your anger.
Cure cancer and keep it to yourself.
Don't spread a word of it. Walk
through hospital wards beaming.
Pop GET WELL balloons
while eating microwave popcorn.
Remind patients they are kernels.

5.

Enslave pandas. They're so delicate,
you know they shouldn't exist. Wear
them down to pads, monochromatic nubs.
Serve them as steaks at a beachside
stand. Slather yours in marinade.

6.

Set bonfires that will glow
and grow so slowly they will
get noticed only when you are ready
to have people notice them.

7.

Ruin a sunset.

8.

Puke in that Coach purse. You know the one.
It belongs to that girl
from that place, gold wallpaper
in the bathroom, talking
ads in the stalls to distract you
from a steady stream. Remember her,
a tipsy slit of flesh and perfume
visible through a crack
in the stall door. Between
swipes of gloss, she told the mirror
your shoes made her nauseous.

Put your finger down your throat,
think about how cheap you are.
Remember smells: brushed leather and urine,
tangy spice, white sugary arrogance.
Do it. Make yourself do it. Haul up
that chicken quesadilla, soak the logo
before she un-passes out,
before that guy in the G-Star jeans
removes his hand from her bra cup.

9.

Draw pictures
of everyone you've known
and wanted to forget.
Use pastels. Keep a fresh box
in the kitchen drawer.
After you've expertly rendered
each haircut, weak jaw,
slipped wit in jellied eyes,
apply your fist
wet with pink smears,
your own saliva. Hand them out
to people in the street.
ask them to point out
faults in your tribute, coerce them
into agreement, that seeing
how these people hurt you,
these wilted pages
should be destroyed.

10.

Stay focussed. See
outbursts through.
Let your anger roll
over skin cells, crackle
through synapses. Do not
regulate breathing. Do not
let your body slow. Do not
rest. Your blood should reach
a rolling boil.

Do not.

This is your rage meditation.

It *Affects* MEMORY

Throw myself in the river,
he says, *might as well.*
He doesn't remember her,
that he likes
potatoes mashed, cool walks.
He doesn't know
that he's grown out of getting this angry,
mid-century rage, king of the castle,
master breadwinner.

Without memory
he thinks suicide, dark things he'd
imagined were for pussies: feelings,
help, mental fortitude, tears.
Says the word "kill,"
says his wife is the other one,
says he needs to go to his other house.
Everything is other.

He made it through
Christmas Eve, Christmas Day,
Boxing Day. The Cold War.
He made it through
heavy meals, hours
at the office, alpha nights
sending teen daughters
to bed before dusk, telling
jokes, solid embraces, necessary
muskrat murder, retirement,
yardwork, yardwork, yardwork,
renovation.

Each day, little bits
flitter away, stories blend.
That's how he kept us fooled
for so long. Stories
what he remembers:
the Sidehill Gouger, the fist fight
at his father's funeral,
puking at the curling rink.

He says, *Remember*. He says, *I hurt*.
He says, *I might hurt her*. He says he needs
to hurt himself. *Might as well*, he says.
He tells a story that trails off,
a sloppy ending.

TAKE *the* Happiness LEVEL™ *quiz*

It's been said that happiness can't be measured. People who posit this idea are quitters and haters, perpetrators of self-doubt and unhappiness. Simply answer this quiz, then add up your score and discover the depth of your Happiness Level™.

1 Do you dream of imagined disagreements?
☹**Yes** = –5 ☺**No** = +2

2 Have you ever reprimanded someone for using the phrase "It is what it is" at a high-end cocktail lounge?
☺**Yes** = +5 ☹**No** = –1

3 Do you ever describe yourself as someone attuned to the mysteries of the heart?
☺**Yes** = +3 ☹**No** = –3

4 Can you remember a time when you felt ultimate satisfaction while others around you struggled with discomfort?
☺**Yes** = +2 ☹**No** = –5

5 Have you scheduled an emotional checkup only to discover you were too afraid to complete the examination and had to sneak out of the doctor's office, shaking and weary?
☹**Yes** = –3 ☺**No** = +3

☺ *Results* ☹

Negative Happiness Level™ Points UNHAPPY
Instruction: Reassess your comprehension of basic joy principles. Draw "!" on a blackboard.

1–5 Happiness Level™ Points HAPPYISH
Instruction: Practise smiling at strangers. Record their reactions.

6–10 Happiness Level™ Points HAPPY
Instruction: Clear your home of precious metals. Store them with your oldest relative.

11–15 Happiness Level™ Points HAPPY MASTER
Instruction: Develop your own happiness program. Teach others. Spread smugness.

HOW TO
be *Happy*

Happiness is a restful bliss. When you're happy, troubles cease to harass you. In order to achieve successful happiness, you must undergo rigorous training governed by a set of detailed instructions. Read through these directions carefully. Do not let your own happiness fail you again, as it has so many times before. Embrace the following directions for happiness and you will move in the direction of happiness.

1.

Secure future happiness.
Make a down payment
on a storage unit. Keep
your possessions at home, shop
for sturdy wood frames,
a top-of-the-line toaster oven,
Egyptian cotton, whimsical
Bunnykins dishware, a hammock.
Don't forget soft lighting,
Wi-Fi connection, rat poison.
Design a lush hideaway,
a placeholder, so you'll know
after the breakup
no division of goods
but a separation. You can give
the one you thought you wanted
objects, somewhere to be.

2.

Win an argument.

3.

Make a list of promises
to yourself, indulgences.
Start with the installation
of whirlpool jets, heated tiles,
glamour-range chrome fixtures.
Select photographs, black-and-white
rubber ducks in wheat fields, hang
sage towels, air plants, a list of rules.
Sit in your refurbished tub,
drink sparkling Riesling,
tip a crystal flute, feel
bubbles wash your throat,
prickle your skin.
Soak up this follow-through
to remind yourself
of past promises
broken.

4.

Invite controversy
in a food court. Rally
teenaged burger-slingers, microwave chefs
to abandon soft-serve, noodle bowls.
Arm them with plastic forks, buoyancy,
lead them to the nearest park.
On the count of three, have them
plunge prongs into dirt. Revel
in their collective
sigh.

5.

Camp out
beside a pop machine
at the bus station. Offer
quarters to travellers.
Let them enjoy
sugar without judgment.

6.

Buy a billboard
to promote yourself.
Advertise your assets:
knife skills, commendable grooming,
knows the difference
between astrology and astronomy,
owns semi-formal attire,
won Most Enthusiastic Youth Bowler
three years in a row.
Save room for larger font
that reads:

MAKES A GREAT BEST FRIEND

Paid in print is truth.
Words hover below your face,
digitally retouched to perfection.

7.

Reconstruct your favourite
masturbatory materials. For a week
work as if this is your full-time job.
Craft a wall of yearbook photos, stolen trinkets,
underwear, rubber bracelets,
catalogue cut-outs. Force yourself
to remember details, to render these elements
with care, as though each is a neglected child.

8.

Train yourself to ignore
your despondent teen, disloyal dog,
spouse submerged in self-doubt,
depression, and online blackjack.
Focus on your own changes,
desire to trade minivan for MINI Cooper,
craigslist, mild activism, a taste for the future.
Don't accept your inability to return,
former self retired. Shuffle through
fluctuations in feeling.

9.

Develop your own diet,
restrict lean meats, sugar substitutes,
seeded bread, sports drinks.
Eat pale foods, dye every crumb
Blue No. 2 to match
your worn-in jeans. Tell people
you're allergic to spirulina,
flaxseed, dopamine reuptake inhibitors.
At midnight, salt leftover french fries,
eat at a vanity, watch
your sapphire mouth.

10.

Wear bare legs
in the cold.
Stand against
weather, moisture.
Carouse in
rush of chill.
Red welts
badges of honour.

Step-by-Step INSTRUCTION
FOLDING

Don't listen to those who tell you to beware of acts that are habit forming. That attitude crushes opportunities. Allow compulsions into your life.

---

1. Education

She was a good student. Mastered technique, learned to make a pair of boot-cuts look pristine. Another for T-shirts. Yet another, different, equally symmetrical method for turtlenecks. Sometimes you need the logo to show. Sometimes a pocket must appear to call out loud to strangers. Cardigans, button-downs, tank tops, shorts – clothes as shapes, squares, rectangles, and trapezoids. Sharp corners pinched from the soft edges of cotton. But this is all protocol. Techniques thought up in a boardroom to regulate standards. It is not a way of life. She quit years ago, finished her degree, married, made herself her own.

2. Practice

They haunt her. Lessons she should have left behind along with her name-tag pulse on her brain. At home, she refolds her husband's underwear, unrolls them, and ensures the seams meet up at right corners. Once, she took apart the chest of drawers to see if there was a way to make her wardrobe more visible to passersby. Dinner guests on their way to the bathroom might see her flannel pyjamas in a new light. Sleepwear that ended up in a pile on the floor gave the opposite impression. It takes her fifteen seconds to perfect-fold a pair of jeans, ten for shirts, twenty-three for bulky winter sweaters. On laundry days, she has to shower after all the garments are stored in compact layers. She works so fast, sweat drips onto the fabric softener–scented clothes she has to wash-dry-fold all over again.

3. Second Nature

She always shops alone. Takes time to reconstruct at least one pile per store. Clerks stare at her, but she believes it's in disbelief. How could a layperson be so competent? When she brings home new purchases, she studies each arm-to-torso ratio, checks the folding technique as she unpacks each item to discover if there are new ways to tuck hems, maintain pleats, create symmetry. On the couch, she brings a sleeve across to meet the other, runs a finger along the fabric to see if the edges match, examines the fibres. Throw pillows are strewn on the floor, and a towel from her morning shower is draped across the back of a chair. These are things she'll get to later. She releases the sleeve and starts again, matches cuff to armpit seam, does the same with the other, whips cloth over and under. With delicate precision, she repeats the process until her hands are mechanized, trained to create that perfect fold.

Admission

There's no real thing called silence, a cold crust, icy snow of youth. Even then, follicles rustled below skin's surface. Dormant shards. Usually I shave, scrape away bristles, hard evidence. Addicted to lightness, trade flesh for silk, quiet. But I can stop. Refuse hair removal. Feel roots gain strength, shimmery hair everywhere. This is it. These dead cells make music as they push through skin, they chime. They create a core ringing. Soft bells rattle calves, thighs. Let it take over, remove doubt that I'm human, alive. Grow like leaves on twigs. Stand the weight, struggle with raucous potency. Snap them off. I can always start fresh. Keep smooth for a stint. Then grow.

TEST *your*
Guilt *Index*™

Escalation of guilt can be determined by comparing your levels against those in this index. Levels cannot be achieved simply, and skipping steps is sometimes necessary to successfully approach Guilt Nirvana.

Guilty Pleasure – What any untrained person feels. Infant-level guilt. Claim it doesn't exist. Remain adamant.

Lies – What you tell yourself to facilitate guilt. What you tell others to increase guilt. A way of living that emboldens you, but also shames.

Unfulfilled Expectations – What you create when you set goals.

Ignore – What you do to make things easier.

Neglect – What you try to do until it becomes natural not to do anything. This is a stepsibling to Ignore. These together complete a vivid picture of median-level guilt.

Thoughtlessness – What you begin to understand as something greater than thoughts. A transcendence. Don't stop thinking. Defend yourself.

Guilt Trip – What you achieve in higher levels of guilt. Ascension to a new emotional plane. The feeling of floating above those you've neglected.

Regret – What you power towards. Where you rest.

HOW to *be* Guilty

Guilt is misunderstood. These pages will reveal the true nature of guilt. You will learn to feel as if you've done something wrong, done someone wrong, done something to damage your humanity. Guilt is human. That feeling – stuck plugs in your alveoli – signals to you that you are alive. Each hard exhale, deep throttle at inhalation, is a sign that you have felt fondness and have felt betrayed, that you have gone against expectation and it turned out to be a mistake, that you have harmed or crushed, impaired or maimed.

This guide will allow you to engage with guilt in many different scenarios, gauge your progress, and compare your Guilt levels with the patented Guilt Index™.

Keep your brain sharp. Do not try to escape the rigours of guilt training. Do not stabilize your guilt. It must constantly move and change. Time heals guilt. To maintain a steady level it must alter, flip, and surprise. The process never ends.

Begin.

1.

Cancel
your cable
subscription.
Set a PVR
to capture
episodes that
never air.
Black screen,

blank

hours.

Watch.

2.

Examine guilt
in the vanity.
How it brings out
green iris flecks,
smooths and distinguishes the jawline,
highlights, heightens
cheekbones
in halogen glow.
Closes pores
like mortar.

Embrace
this make-over.
Don't question why
it looks so good on you.

3.

Don't admit
you've found
new joys. Sit
with a cappuccino
near a clinic –
falsely humble.

The worst thing in the face
of others' unhappiness is
your happiness.

4.

Commit a crime.
Don't speed or shoplift,
actions explained away.
Creep
into the loft
of your first love.
Not the one who left
gloves on the front seat
as incentive to return
for minivan make-outs. Not the one
with the robot backpack,
not the one with the high arches,
the one with nubbed fingers
working overtime all over you,
the one who caught colds,
the one who let you wait
until it was obvious you
would be alone forever,
you know, the one
who made you.
The one.
Arrive mid-morning,
set hair traps in the drain,
wait a week, return.
Remove your first love's
lover's hair, shape a body,
perfect and lovable, soft.
Return it to their shared bathroom
newly formed.
Take their
lubricant.
Breaking and entering
relieves broken
feelings.

5.

Don't feel sorry
for someone else's illness.
Feel sorry for yourself
for having to be around.

6.

Forget to put the dog out,
your anniversary,
the day your aunt died. Let
ways of seeing turn to ignorance,
ask a close friend for reminders.
Let neglect fester
like an infected wound.

7.

Waste good food.

8.

Keep your story straight,
relay few, fictive details
over days, weeks, months:
a hotel lobby,
a bruise, a hickey,
a handicapped stall, breath
mints, a phone number,
agenda, a taste for kale,
ticket stub, dryer sheets.
After these reveals,
wake your partner
with cries in the night.

9.

Reject an heirloom.

10.

Run, pound uphill,
past trails, ignore
natural beauty, crest,
concrete, sidestep,
swipe, thunder ahead
of walkers, the homeless,
strollers, and leashes.
At the apex
of a covered parkade,
take a painful breath,
each prickle a swallow
of ticketed air.

KICK

At 4:00 a.m. you kick me awake, foot to nose. I stumble through sheets, push them off, and down the bed I see you're not right. Body opposite mine, upside-down, everything. On the floor, your flannel pants a crumpled version of your legs. Kicked, too, a victim of feet. Unable to get comfortable, I see. Your naked body, brown, specked with dark hair, and there in the middle of it all, like someone had wiped it off like a spot of dirt, your penis, missing. A dome of flesh. I trace the curve of it with my fingertips, too curious to wake you. In moments like this, it doesn't matter if I'm in a dream or not. Hand cupped around your Ken-doll shape, I think about the time I made you angry in the fitting room at the department store. Proud of your choice, as always, you took my comment as bad feelings. It was no one's fault that the jeans made it look like you were small. With a whip of your arm, you slammed the door and I stood outside with the underpaid employee who looked at me like I might be the devil. But now, there's nothing up front. You don't move when I touch it, so I prod your skin, try to make you kick, react, whisper, anything. Still as a rock, you lick your lips once. I turn away and hope nothing has changed by morning.

Paper

Glossy, could be a distraction. But no. This is respectable gloss, the kind you see slotted in a magazine rack in someone's bathroom and feel giddy, glad your shit will mix with theirs. For the low cost of a subscription, we can enjoy monthly trips to lands where we project, where people are desperate or magical or soulful. As ass warms seat, we hold the whole world. Deserts spread like taffy. Barges of refuse. Sharks, shrimps, shamans, shredded lettuce in a wooden bowl. And then we turn the page. A child sees her own face in the glassy silver of a balloon. Unlike us, when we wash our hands in front of the mirror, wiped and spent, body-shamed, she's tiny, cute, like there's nothing wrong with her. Except there might be. Except her whole self could float away, body light as a slip of paper. One helium inhale to levitate, separate her from shiny, glossy plastic. Except we don't know. Except when we look, all we see are the whites of our eyes reflected in the sheen of paper.

This Guide
Includes
Thrilling Bonus
Features

SAD **LIBS**

SAD WORDS
GUIDE

Exciting *and* truthful
sad-sack, *transformation*
TESTIMONIALS

HOW TO *be* *Sad*

Sadness lives in many places: city parks, gymnasiums, mountaintops, your mom's house, your breastbone. You carry it around with you in a fanny pack, and yet, do you make sad work for you? Throughout this guide you'll find a system that works, a system of unending ways of sadness. Don't let sadness become a secondary emotion. Take control and make your sadness work for you.

At the end of this twelve-step manual, you'll find a new emotion living inside you, a sadder, better sadness. Call it "friend." Make it sing show tunes with you. Or metal ballads. Or *Mellon Collie and the Infinite Sadness*. Just know that this new emotion companion will always be with you, because you'll have mastered the art of how to be sad.

1.

Make a mixed tape,
on a real cassette. String together
analog heartbreak strung together.

Spend days in a garage workshop
just to discover the problem inside
that pink ghetto blaster
is that you can't fix it
after throwing it
                    down

                            two
            flights
of stairs.

Halve the plastic casing, unwind
the sheen of tape, wrap thin songs
around your naked body,
feel those words, soft rhythms,
manipulative voices. They surround you.
Feel songs as though they were hands
set to make you remember
what it's like to be comforted.

2.

Call every relationship an accident,
even the ones you calculated, like geometry,
shaped, angled at the right degree to make falling
easy, because you could do it into another person,
someone's volume to hold you. Realize
theorems are a mishap.

TESTIMONIAL

I like the way my body operates.
Softer than a Q-tip rims the
ear, more satisfying, too, now
I realize. I feel it. No theory, an
honest transformation. I've had
cotton lost, a wad trapped so
hard, been unable to dislodge.
The hurt made me numb. I've
gained control over all my
orifices, over organs, over fluids.
Tears like an enema.

– Jerry
Hoople, North Dakota

3.

Stalk the lanky boy
from the bakery. Follow
his arms as they rotate sheets of dough,
mimic his movements, sprinkle flour
in your skin creases.

At night, crawl onto the kitchen floor,
cuddle a bag of day-old dinner rolls.

4.

Even though
you have nowhere to wear them,
buy a shirt in a flattering shape
in every colour.

When you unload
the shopping bag at home,
think only
about how
you have nowhere to wear them.

5.

Make a tiny replica of your home
under the bed. With attention to detail,
hang photographs from the metal frame,
measure distance between rugs, chairs, empty bottles
overflowing the recycling bin. Invite old friends over.
Serve them leftovers in your dollhouse living room.
When they demand garnish, give them handfuls
of chip crumbs. Sweep a palm full of dust for dessert.

6.

Rub garlic on your fingers. Snap
bulbs, rotate raw cloves until
scent absorbs deep into print grooves, until
a cartoon stink is achieved. Wear delicate fabrics,
look vulnerable, as though a small child
could tear your shirt from your chest with a tiny fist.
Don't wear red. Or a hat. Rub fingers
into your eyeballs before you enter the coffee shop
where you broke someone's spirit. Grind the sting,
fingertips to cornea, until
you can barely see. Sob until
the barista offers you a free latte.

7.

Join a parade, with a renegade float,
helium balloons, plushy animal –
suited toddlers, candy-coloured
backdrop. Layer T-shirts:

I'm With Stupid ☞
My Other Mother Is a MILF
Did I Do That?
FBI (Female Body Inspector)

Insist iron-on statements
are arbiters of truth.

Climb wire, plaster, pastel
to the top.
Scream into the mic:

No one told me there would be ugly people here!

Over
and over
until the assembled crowd
boos you for endless city blocks,
children soak their fluff
in spitty screams.

8.

Create strict rules
to govern sadness.
Allow yourself to cry only
if you complete levels of video games,
if you win arguments in grocery lines,
if your fingers
are curled into claws.

TESTIMONIAL

Vodka was only part of the
answer, helped me solve the
problem of how to stay chilled,
keep my emotions crisp. The
rest came from careful study:
mirrors, shop clerks, guys I'd
want to wake up with only in
the glory of a snowstorm.

– Tim
Drumheller, Alberta

9.

Make sadness about winning. Trophies,
gold men in bowling shoes, ribbons
pinned on shirt fronts, stars on papers
on fridges with magnets that advertise
things a sad person doesn't care about:
insurance, travel agents, transmission
repair, family-sized fried chicken meals
with gelatinous dips and pulpy slaw.

10.

Care about the environment.

11.

After the longest span of sadness,
sew all your used handkerchiefs together,
spread tears and snot and stiff cotton
in the highest-density park.
Picnic with tourists.

12.

Don't underestimate your sadness.
Commission a plaque that reveals
your saddest desire. Pay the guy
in the basement of the mall
to engrave your dreams
in black metal bound to semigloss cherry.
Mount your unattained aspirations
on a street lamp on the busiest corner in town.

TESTIMONIAL

She thought I killed our
friendship, not sure if mercy
factors in. She didn't want to
explore sadness, kept lines
of communication open,
crocheted pot holders. So much
connectivity. I learned to untie,
leave threads behind, cut holes.
Shred. To unravel was to satisfy.
Not everyone knows it's as
painful to ditch as be ditched,
that sorrow in leaving.

– Trish
Fruitvale, British Columbia

SAD LIBS

1.

_____
TITLE

Couch Potato _____,
VERB

but _____ honours radiance. No
NOUN

_____ is a standing lamp,
NOUN

a _____ light. That's why
ADJECTIVE

she _____ the throw pillow,
VERB

painted one wall _____,
COLOUR

and changed the order of the shelf

to match her sadness. Nothing

is brighter than _____,
NOUN

because she only sees herself

reflected in the dark _____.
NOUN

84

SAD LIBS

2.

_____
TITLE

What?

_____
NOUN

_____
NOUN

Oh.

_____
NOUN

_____
NOUN

No.

SAD WORDS

Corn chips.

Fluke.

Notice.

Stepladder.

Dockers.

Honour.

Shatter.

Acronym.

Estimate.

Creature
COMFORTS

It's just sort of an interesting phenomenon.
Everybody's linked to it. I don't think it's a
particularly remarkable video. I think it's cute.

– Cynthia Holmes, *CBC News*, Tuesday, April 3,
   2007, commenting on her "Otters holding hands"
   YouTube video uploaded March 19, 2007

Celebrity **Otter** *Nyac*

Nyac rose above her celebrity.
She suffered fools
when she should
have given them the finger,
covered her eyes to block out idiots,
a barrage of khaki pants, Orange Crush–
stained lips of drippy children,
dads checking out
trainer's ass
bent
      over her
           pool.
Hardly insulting, it was adorable.
So fucking adorable, that she could be
so patient.

Nyac rose above her celebrity,
could have shown up
Angelina on a red carpet
with a dip and a swirl, a paw to her cheek.
Even though she never once
heard Brad's voice
expound on Frank Gehry,
motorcycles, the perfect
stubble, she looked good in the glossies.
She held hands in public,
had the same partner for years.

Celebrity **Otter** *Nyac*

Rest in peace, Nyac! i'm happy you could finish your life in
a nice place, safe from the stupidity of some humans ...

— "clairenunavut," comment posted May 2011
on "nyac the otter tribute"
YouTube video uploaded October 2, 2008

Before social media, you were a nobody.
Snuffed and rafted with your family in open water
as though there was no other way,
as though in twenty years you would not be
a poster child for tragedy and tourism.
Your light fur, golden, a shade women pay
top dollar to achieve in layers of ammonia
and petroleum,
hours in a stylist's chair.

From slicked black, snout not even visible,
to picture-perfect, made for advertisements, plush toys, mugs.
Fur-print tote bags instead of torn from your flesh.
You had the right story, a TV movie starring
Jennifer Love Hewitt, that you overcame with
take-a-look-at-me-now appeal. You were a girl fished
from a well, a kidnapping survivor, a wartorn orphan,
a slim pup reborn in oil.

Celebrity Otter Milo

chemotherapy for a rodent …???? bizarre

– "Terdherder," comment posted
January 12, 2012, on "Celebrity sea otter
dies at Vancouver Aquarium after six-month
battle with lymphoma," *National Post*

He makes lymphoma
seem like a lollipop flavour
under aquarium supervision,
breaks from treatment to brush
his loose coat, massage through
to his skin,   swims in blue pools
    back from the crowd,
like his aqua-coloured home,
everything he knows
looks like a late-sixties bathroom
someone means to renovate.
Cells divide as fast
as YouTube views accumulate.
Same technology used
at Children's Hospital,
that other place of
adorable sadness.

He lost Nyac three years ago.
He was her boy toy, eleven years younger,
good as any Beverly Hills
housewife. A pool boy.
Unlike humans, he plays well
into twilight years, into times
when bones and arteries
are more like accessories,
not utilitarian. Twelve is probably
seventy in otter years.

An old man at the bowling alley
told me most males pass
within nine and a half months
of losing a spouse.

He didn't get a single strike
that afternoon, forearms
worn from his own wife's
early-morning instruction.
Weed, mow, break down
that door I wanted you
to build three years ago.

Like an ailing politician, we weep
for Milo, hold vigils
on the Internet. I advise
we make small shrines in our homes:
tasteful glitter pens, foam core,
fake candles, ceramic replicas
looted from the gift shop.

The newscaster disagrees,
advocates for time spent
outdoors, not thinking
about the otter. Turns out
no one listens to me.

Still we all come back
to his and hers, paws together,
rescued. On glowing screens
we watch, listen
to visitors coo and awe
over nature's basest connection.

I advise substitution:
a Robert Palmer soundtrack,
or Roxette. Do with that
what you will.

Each view gives the world
cute chemotherapy.

Celebrity **Otters** *Nyac* and *Milo*

For Cynara

Peacocks roam
in colour, elegant struts
through rose garden,
in a park in a rain forest,
ritzy cultivation.

They have their ways –
cute paws grope, tear
sophisticated neck from body.
The two of them wrench
until breast bursts, rusty
guts, pink ribs, against
blue, green, a natural
feast, multicoloured meal.
Mouthfuls of dry fowl.

Feathered tail
discarded, no accessory,
no boa. Would project
a haughty image;
doesn't fit
their aesthetic.

This is raw.

No white tablecloth,
no attempt to escape
waiting lenses, paparazzi,
just this unexpected
delicacy. They deserve
to gorge on exotic fare. Almost
as tasty as the Fat Duck.
Blumenthal would appreciate
their expanded mustelid palates.

Whiskered cheeks
adorned with jewel-toned tufts,
chest plates heaped with navy
morsels, teeth stained red, lipstick
traces of vibrant
acts of biological wonder.

Treated to something
no one thought existed:
high-end fast food.

Bold taste, easily delivered.

Celebrity **Otter**s
Nyac and *Milo* and *Elfin*

For Annabel

They're always watched. During business hours or not, the constant otter cam to capture feats of whimsy. They appear in little windows on computers, crack spreadsheets, task lists, meeting notes. Or late at night, virtual companions. They swish and swirl, dive, sleep, groom fur, fur, fur, face, leave frame. Sometimes there are three of them together. There has to be a hanger-on, entourage of one. Families visit marine exhibits to capture the best video footage on a day like today, sky like unwashed bedsheets, threat of rain, no glare from above. These creatures hurl themselves in front of crowds, celebrities with nothing to lose, protected by glass and stone, their animal urges. Milo butts her, she sways to meet him, flits away. He nips, whips leatherette flesh of Nyac's nose until it's raw, meaty, and she rolls with it, bumps against him; it sticks. They multi-task, thrust, and swim. Strokes missed and caught, more pushes, bites, her face held under water. Joyful. Dangerous. Some would call it rough. Yet Nyac yawns, slow-paddles, eyes tight. In a crook of sculpted rock, Elfin pumps his paw against his rosy protrusion. No one covers the eyes of kids. Hey, kids! Nature's majesty. Red lights flash and blink, lenses trained on this display. They continue to romp. No one breaks the mood to set a tripod, magic stays alive.

Celebrity **Otters**
Elfin and *Tanu*

Dear Elfin

> *Why can't you make peace and get along with others? Tanu,*
> *the poor girl, needs your friendship after Milo died. She*
> *seems just to have realized that Milo will never come back.*

Milo, I love you forever …

– "proialee," comment posted May 2012 on
"nyac the otter tribute" YouTube video

Can't recast
even though
they look like
clones of cute.

Can't recreate magic.

It doesn't work that way.

No one has anything to say.

This show will probably
be cancelled.

Like

39 comments
1 comment
1 comment
0 comments
0 comments
0 comments
0 comments
0 comments

Compare
18,154,119 views

to

74,560 views
330 views
169 views
50 views
44 views
25 views
22 views
5 views

Celebrity **Otters** Us

Otters are just like us!

They eat. They fuck. They cower. They whine. They play. They nap.
They groom. They eat. They groom. They eat. They groom. They fuck.
They want to float endlessly in the wide-open sea. They eat. They groom.
They eat. They sleep. They eat.

EARTH *Day*
/ **Easter**

Dry, her grey whale flesh and the sand that the spring winds coated her in. Grains shake from her skin, moisture leaves her body. Like a child opening her hand over a toy in a sandbox, a shower of dirt. Sun behind clouds, her skin changes texture, warps. Stuck on this beach, nowhere to go, at first because she didn't know how, the tide uncooperative, but then because she is dead. Whales beach here so often I'm surprised no one has invented a whale Zamboni to clear them away.

After she's really dried up and the looky-loos have gawked, she's cut open. Whether the exam is for the greater good of sea science or just because it's human nature to want to see the innards of a dead thing washed up where people usually eat popsicles. Inside her the expected kelp and krill, and an unwelcome lost and found. A purse, a plastic cup, a grocery bag, sweatpants, a pack of gum. *People* magazine. Surgical gloves. Undigested toys. A green skipping rope suctioned to her stomach lining. No one claims these lost possessions, things easily replaced after a half-hour at the mall.

Early morning in a cupcake dress and sneakers, a plastic, pastel skipping rope nestled in the synthetic grass of an Easter basket. Colours that mean things are changing to stimulating brightness, to pops in front of my eyes that mean I can be outside without my coat on. Skin crisped by sun, stung by chill breezes I pretend not to care about because it's more important to be outside, tossing the rope over my head, and jumping, to hear that satisfying clap of plastic against the driveway as I sing:

> *A sailor went to sea sea sea*
> *To see what he could see see see*
> *But all that he could see see see*
> *Was the bottom of the deep blue sea sea sea*

Each repetition of "see" or "sea" is supposed to speed up, make you jump faster, and I do, less than a second of rubber soles against concrete, I whip the rope, wrench my wrists, pummel this new thing until my breath jumbles the song in my mouth and I have to stop. Rest my furious drive, pick up the rope. I see a frayed gash in the curve of plastic. I had broken through the surface, ruined it. Cross-legged I sit, curl, and uncurl the cut rope around my fingers.

Spider

She doesn't write web messages,
too insecure to communicate
with complex language. Limbs
struggle to cling, slip, dangle.
All crooked climbs
back up to the light fixture.
She looks like clumped hair,
fished from the drain.

Swings from her shabby
strands, body mousy, like a bad dye job,
home-kit streaks with flimsy gloves.
Though she crawled out of the spout
she looks homemade, crafted
in art therapy. Eight toothpicks
snapped, hot-glued
to a hollow bead of glass.

She limps along, must rest
at intervals to avoid what
I can only assume to be
spider panting. No food
webbed near her, nothing
for days but heat from a bulb.
She'll burn up by morning,
flamed by 60 watts
because I always leave
the bathroom light on.

BULL

I've been listening to him make a lusty ruckus for weeks. He storms the field below our house. I fill a glass and wait for you to hear. Condensation on my hand, I brush static from my skirt. You didn't hear when I tore the shower curtain from the rod. I know you missed the sound of my heels clacking up the drive after work, me shouting for the flowers to fucking grow already, the whirring sound my head makes when I pass you in the bedroom. I hear the bull bellow. I hear it every day. His voice reaches our house past the field of cows who will all be mounted but not heard. They do not respond to the bull, lost in his bellow.

Bedbug

He's been meaning to think more
about bedbugs. I tell him
they will overcome
our finest cities,
create a socio-economic level,
bring about equality.

Pervasive little monsters, the new
pop culture; science and art working as one.
An enemy of commerce, unless
you exterminate. Poisoners will be our
modern knights, saviours.

He takes an extra-fine rollerball
to my arm. Temporary-tattooed notes
and diagrams; later, we come to conclusions
about what they mean for the future,
plan our attack, our message.

We'll gather
as many as we can,
fill a ten-storey
Plexiglas sculpture
of the Statue of Liberty
with their red bodies, a mass of scabs in motion,
tour from the Eastern Seaboard, through
the Midwest, the forests of the Pacific Northwest.
Sealed and visible, locked up
until their lifecycle ends,
we watch them die.

This might only strengthen
their resolve, more determined
in their biological urge
to suck and drain until we're all
forced from the streets, back
further and further
until we're wild.

THE GIRL*with* the
Chinese-Character-She-Thinks-Means-Dragon Tattoo

Your small dog holds more
sartorial sway than I ever will
by virtue of her clothing budget.
So easy to afford Burberry
when the amount of fabric
to clothe a body
would barely cover half
my thigh, easier to achieve
a blowout
with hair that covers
less surface area than my shin.

Your small dog's carrier
matches her jacket, and the leash
is buttery leather, gold-plated,
engraved with your
small dog's name and Michael Kors
which would be a fine name
for a small dog, but not for one
with such luscious hair.

Perhaps I don't understand the importance
of small dogs, their secret generosity,
gentle hum of midnight wisdom. Their compact
power an asset. I see the way you tote your small dog
like a bedazzled hand grenade.

And still, your small dog swims in extra-small
while I squeeze into medium. And no one
carries me to the toilet if it's cold and
I can't hold in my morning pee.

THE *saddest person* in the **ROOM**

Holds a plastic cup with his left hand,
the right busy tapping out a rhythm on
that cup. Being around these arty types makes him
nervous, question gatherings. He tries
to appear natural, as if he could write legibly
if asked to document the evening on a cocktail napkin.
Each piece in the gallery whispered about, held up
as an example of importance.

The saddest person does not want to answer
to people who want to shape his taste, put
pretension on a pedestal. He wants to push
the girls who've filled the room with "like," push them
off the fire escape into the garbage dumpsters. He wants
retirees to tell him of the glory days, how many cents
a decent-sized turkey used to cost. He wants to clear the gallery
and build a volcano out of wire and plaster of Paris.

Acknowledgements

I would like to thank Garry Thomas Morse for his sharp editorial insight, support, and for "getting it." I'd like to extend thanks to Ann-Marie Metten, Les Smith, and Greg Gibson for all their help and to everyone else at Talonbooks for being so darn lovely.

Special thanks to my writing group, The Lyin' Bastards: Sally Breen, Keri Korteling, Nancy Lee, Judy McFarlane, Denise Ryan, Carol Shaben, and John Vigna. You fine people have been essential to my writing life; you have sated me with many bottles of wine, tasty cheeses, and baked goods; and you have indulged my many beauty- and fashion-related tangents.

Thanks and big love to the following friends who helped shape this book with their encouragement, keen eyes, smarts, and tender and tough love: Jag Dost, Cynara Geissler, Alana Green, Laura Matwichuk, Roxan Marucot, Kellee Ngan, Sheryda Warrener, and Daniel Zomparelli. You've all done more for me than you'll ever know.

I'd like to thank Cynthia Holmes for filming Nyac and Milo holding hands at the Vancouver Aquarium and uploading her video to YouTube. Without it, there would be no meme, no comments, and no poems. Another thank-you to all the bookstores I've ever worked in for giving me the opportunity to observe and analyze so many self-help sections.

Thanks to my family, especially my parents, Henry and Teri Del Bucchia, for their support and love, and my brother, Andrew Del Bucchia. You're all the reason I see humour in the poetry of this ridiculous world.

And of course thanks to Jason. For so much. Love you.

Everyone listed here has not only made this manuscript better, but my life too. These people are the best.

Photo by RUTH SKINNER
Happy Otter by ALANA GREEN

Dina Del Bucchia was born in the Trail regional hospital and grew up in the small village of Fruitvale, British Columbia. Most of her working life has been spent in bookstores, both independent and big box. She writes for *Canada Arts Connect* magazine, and her writing has appeared in literary publications across Canada, and as art in the Old Friends' exhibition *Funny Business* (Gallery Atsui, Vancouver, 2010). A literary-event coordinator and host, she also performed a one-woman show at the 2005 Vancouver International Fringe Festival. She has taught creative writing to children and teens at the Vancouver Public Library and as part of the Vancouver Biennale's Big Ideas program, and she holds an MFA in creative writing from the University of British Columbia. Del Bucchia was a finalist for the 2012 RBC Bronwen Wallace Award for Emerging Writers. She lives in Vancouver.